Begin at Once

Begin at Once

Beth Baruch Joselow

chax press
tucson 2007

Printed in the United States of America

Chax Press / 101 W. Sixth Street / Tucson, AZ 85701-1000 / USA

ISBN 978-065-925904-65-2

The author would like to acknowledge with gratitude the publications in which some of these poems first appeared. Many thanks to the editors: Charles Alexander, Jules Boykoff, Kaia Sand, Buck Downs, Cathy Eisenhower, Lorraine Graham, Nigel Hinshelwood, Leslie Scalapino, and Mark Wallace, for their support.

"Query," "Jackpot!," "Change at the Gate" and "When We Were Violent" appeared in the chapbook, *The Bottleneck,* published by Interrupting Cow, Washington, DC.

Self Regard was first published as a chapbook by Chax Press.

"Smoking" first appeared in a limited edition set of letterpress postcards edited and published by Buck Downs at Pyramid Atlantic.

"Stands (Adams Morgan)" appeared in *Membrane.*

"Tantrum" appeared in *The Tangent.*

"We Startle Things" was published in *Enough.*

for Tom Mandel

CONTENTS

ONE

Au Lecteur

The reader likes you to tell him/her what
he/she already knows.
— Alice Notley

Do you have days when you don't feel well?
Do you have days?

I worked on my hand
writing until it was perfect

in the same sense,
I preferred it as it was,

had always been; the years
have softened some

of the lines and broken others,
no need to feel—

Get! Get to the other side:
a decade, a mirror, a walled garden,
hokey and specific if not perfect.

Does it get any better than this?
Do I have to?

I saw him rotate the handle
in exactly the manner he had been
instructed to employ.
It fit neatly in his palm,
a ball in the outfielder's glove.

As always, you must gradually insist
upon whatever needs to be,
then grow more insistent, more
forgiving.

Query

Why does the guy who's
Staggering keep firing?

People, parts
On the broken street

A wind storm shifts the way
They tell us what to do

It's a story, the only
Way to learn, a parable, a joke

My Romance

Arrives with a rose in its hand, a kind
of rose that dies before you can get it
into water, separates his thoughts
into categories just after he thinks them.

Lust crowds the view. If he had been a famous
collaborator and denied his part,
what happened to his thoughts now confined
to a prison camp with laughter and mad dancing.

***

It is about

Not taking her son's hand, walking but not
taking in a hot day in June, draped
in heavy fabric. His legs appear
as if put on backward.

I see them through two layers of glass doors,
their sound caught in the glass before
it can get to me. If you were a child once
you might remember to trust that gesture.

***

It's all about

A minute ago everybody was sunbathing on the deck.
Inside of me I am inside of you.
Another cinderblock room in Cognito,
Where the popular vacation.

Retreat to gas pipes, water lines, electric
wires. Bury the wires rather than loop them
through the garden. These efforts often
impress us as nervous, for we are so accustomed

About the house

A polish that comes of being touched over and over
again, the ordinary staircase, faced with
the problem of lighting, every nook and corner pure
white. Too much for me. It needs shadows.

***

About (saving) face

Depends on the kindness of strangers.
Follows an assertion in a true medium.
Speech without response
at the level of separation it establishes.

If the Romans had practiced nursing as
contraception, abandonment as a gentle
check on population growth, those nonprolific
couples would not have given up

joyful rediscovery of long-lost
children or lovers, shepherds or –
as a man who buys a girl worries *he*
will have to give *her* up.

These words appear
to exclude any response anywhere,
cannot restore
the "transparency of the code."

The radical alternative lies elsewhere these days.

Attempts to develop an optimistic and offensive position
must be embraced. "Elegance is frigid." Both

men's and women's can shatter the spell of the day.

****

About to orient ourselves, about to
light the stone lantern. Awareness of
the softness and warmth of paper. Guide
the shadows to where the children lean

into the distance, prowling our medicines,
gadgets, religion, art and business,
the conduct of our everyday lives.

Fireworks

Will it rain today?
Will we get wet?

Rivers on your face bearing
the water of life.

Crowded school.
A circular shower room
with forty running girls, the bark
of the teacher a bullet
against tile walls.

Tables where students buss their trays,
warm, stale milk and sour
sponges – so much
for sentimental memory.

The gears don't mesh,
the teeth keep making
dents in the metal
turning fitfully
making an irritating noise,
going nowhere.

Time stacks up
against us; we go faster.

                    *

New house off New Road
and a host of running boys.
Jasmine does not grow here.
Only Holly, Ivy, Rose.

Trillion or Mispillion River
un homage à deux
reckless as necessitated by
the need to know whether
one is alive.

Rain today?
*

Walked into the void
and found everyone there already –
late again.

You don't have to pick up
everything you see in the street, or speak
to everyone who calls.

Adopt a child's point of view, willing
to risk a long fall, jump
from the porch roof – fireworks
hang in the air, melt in the trees.

Hearing bells, watching colors
expand in the night. Headlights
caress the walls of my room,
trains whistle me to sleep.

To Be Private and Not So

To be private and not so
private
to take on silence
or appropriate noise

Remembering his
puzzle
in the shower each morning,
or when looking at a rose
a cartoon, a photo of
his face and someone else's
hands behind him.

Elephants dressed
for the circus, a stupid joke,
a restaurant named
Mrs. Simpson's,
where three streets meet,
plaid and seersucker,
Applejack,
pet names that
make no sense anymore,
lips pursed in a certain way,
my eyes, the shape of my brow.

Grief is a kind of constant
buzz, wearing, and yet
we know a revelation
would be so unrevealing.

This is not identity.
It isn't true, but is
a circumstance that must be
encompassed,
like it or not.

You Don't Have to Like It
You Just Have to Eat It

We were not the kind of people who
cheerfully shouted "hurrah."
                    —Marina Linnik, *Stalin's Ghost*

People who are loud and don't care
who hears what.

She once was mean to him
in an ugly gray-shingled house.

A mean low building
housing a daycare center.

Heavy blocks of stitched together houses
loops of busses
cars beaded with rain on a factory parking lot.

These are your personal belongings,
the tops of buildings obscured by clouds.

The weight of Walnut Bridge, Locust Point,
Bible and book manufacturing.

                    *

Held high in the air
a shaft of wheat, a sheaf of

dried carnations in a blue bottle
centered on a marble counter
cracked and monogrammed.

Why feel fraudulent,
if you've proffered nothing?

More than the show I like
the openings to shows, parts that move very fast,
three-second clips propelled by glimpses
of what I'd like to linger on.

I was lying.

I'm not lying now.

I love to see the building collapse,
I love to see the workman spray
the cement with water,
I love to see the woman smile,
the men look wary,
the Chinese dragon.

I love to be asleep.

*

What a day to be thankful for
grabbing at deadlines.

Weighty thoughts and weightless
Thoughts, almost the same.

An amber flower, a grass green flower
a broom and an expensive ribbon
used to sweep anger aside
tie up loose ends in these last days of the year.

No regrets. *Rien de rien.*

(His images are boring. He strives
for the familiar.)
(Her images are hard to find
in a swamp of mimicry.)

Music takes up room.
Slides and negatives
aspire to miniature housing
but for now they are dense and heavy.

*

Relief pours through
the ceiling like
water from
a broken pump.

Long, sad mistake,
solution reached erroneously.

There is no original, or
it was forged long ago.

Movement between natural things,
washed out, risky.

You don't have to like it.
You just have to eat it.
Why should it matter who you were to them?

*

I am making a survey
of running boys
and what they are running toward.

*

The bull smokes a cigar
as he emerges from the labyrinth.
Need I explain?

Waiting to merge with the stream
of traffic.

Sometimes on my way home I
am indulgent of
meaningless conversations.

I am taking old advice,
feeding my head.

*

A new catalog of roses,
thirty rosebushes in a box
on the front porch
in time for spring,
bare of all but thorns.
I gave them to Rosanne.

I can't seem to keep
it going every day
even in perpetual motion,
even at the level of atoms.

I remember sitting
very still
looking intently at
a mahogony hi-fi cabinet
trying to discern
the motion of its molecules,
certain I could,
if I just kept still enough.

The roses
began to bloom in the box.

*

Leaving a warm house
for another doctor's visit,
a warm house smelling
of toast. The dog
barks,
the children sit soberly
in front of the TV,
their fingerprints
all around the doorknobs.

You keep enlarging your ranks.
I mean I keep enlarging my ranks.
I mean, we do.
All of these children, and friends,
for instance.

Showcased that way they
seem like people other
than the ones we had known
in the smaller house.

We Startle Things

Go into this mediating passage
and throw it another plum.

It seems to belong there,
hanging against an azure sky
riffled with islands.

I left, tucked
straight through the windshield,
painlessly liberated all at once.
The clock on the dash
recorded the hour.

I believe this to be true
although recited from memory,
house of amber with a muddy view.

                    ∧

We startle things
into going, we take over
the path, stride
into the passable
like sheriffs,
without once thinking
of what gets cut off.

I waited on the lip for the last drop,
then the rain stumbled in from the East
and we wound our way down.
At times and in places
like this
even an attempt is commendable.

∧

Some people
need an ambulance
every day of their lives

don't know
which way is up
and even then

Pitch

Full moon has that holy look,
and the sky is back, back.

Long cloud, grey scarf on the bed.

A shepherd, an onion
layer under layer.

Is he on the mezzanine,

the iron stairs,
the sound of his shoes–

bits of gravel and asphalt,
pits in the paving of the alley–

on my knees again.

Self Regard

Reckless intimacy!

Along the coast of abandon
forgotten to respect
a self blocked now

blocked, left wanting
more from close attention
to pride.

Fresh bread and falling water,
a table for one and a fair
degree of wondering

what time it is.
Stop here a minute.
I would rather be alone

with my thoughts, thank you.

Ray knew how to have fun elegantly.
Still, all is not lost.

The restaurant looked so promising
but we should have taken into account
that we were in a small, unknown city.

I stood there for a long time.
Now I've gone past you in a slow
turn. My sights less cluttered,

more centered (energy is still diffuse).

I don't need to keep track
of you the way I once did.

Room after room of all I do not know.
Things you cannot know without
first knowing other things.
The story of Saint Lucy, for example, before I can
understand this Veronese, yet
I have been to Venice many times.

Quickening footsteps on wide oak planks, on palatial
slabs of marble.
The boy's head, hair, lively eyes,

known to me. Can he really
be dead these hundreds of years?
Light enters from the sky and is sufficient.

I have one hour more here.
Water splashes
and plays at the center of circled

columns, the pale
sunlit dome.
Try at least to be charming.

＾ ＾ ＾

I remember when sex defined the nature of everything I did,
informed my vocabulary and syntax when I wasn't looking.
This is still the case but much more subtle, tempered by age
and fulfillment.

"But at night I am just
so tired,
mulling over all the things I would change."

29

"What about *me*? Don't *I* get a hug?"
Should we tell each other
our names, or should we just let it go?

"The working class
and the employing class
have nothing in common."

Its nature is temporary, that's for certain. Now the students all
seem to want the heroes to have feet of clay. The genial com-
poser, the fleet-fingered pianist.

Got off on the wrong foot,
unamplified until the late eighties.

∧ ∧ ∧

Electric motor service and foil to broil in.

Why this and not that?
Why the appeal of Portuguese but not Hungarian?
The house painted pale blue
 looks grim next to the fresh yellow house.

Large, significant structures made of steel
stand beside the railroad tracks.

Cross over a frozen pond that appears to be
something other than water, a gray slurry something.

"That a sacred site can be bartered away just like another piece
of dirt."

Branch and ache.

Loaded with how happy I am to be coming home to you.
Of course I want them to attend to my body,
that transparency.

New badge.

Beside their faces and their perfect coats
no theft takes place.
See all the way through that house

in a sad way. In March the light
along this parallel is still thin.

I began to keep a record, an antidote.

How much

        Once we

        How can

        What will

Between us
Once
We feel
We know

How to enable the melting snow, the return of power.

I walk down the aisle
without my shoes
to watch TV
through the front window
of the neighborhood tavern.

0

Quit smoking at a hockey game when she saw how yellow
the smoke from her cigarette was against the ice.

Such a dark sky tonight in Baltimore.
Graceful bones of her hand flicking past her face,
glimpse of a charming, unselfconscious gesture.

Violet sky still visible.
Dutch neighbors look down into my dining room and see
me at this table.

You are so afraid I don't think of you, but I do.
On the bus in front of the Frick today I remembered
sending you a message. I remembered other efforts.

She may want to look the way she looks yet it seems
a lack of consciousness
to talk in the rhythms
of sporadic shooting breaking out in the suburbs of Beirut.
Designing your life is a luxury.

I have him
fifty cents
because there was no innocence in him.
It was the first day of spring. My children
were wearing funky sunglasses and riding around with the
music
up loud.

Until I feel your body is more
mine than theirs I cannot be
content.

Too much got by me during that time. A sense

of humor entirely lost, so that I could not stop seeing their
joyous coupling when another greener scene was called for.

Should youth ever be denied?
In the orphanage in Serbia the rooms are kept at 55 degrees
so that no child will actually freeze.

Few of our conversations were significant or even personal yet
at one point he did tell me that I did not have to continue to
wear shoes that hurt my feet. I took him at his word and threw
them out, although they were rather new. And on another
occasion he bought me an album he thought I would like, and
I did like it. This was over a period of 20 years.

Cup of coffee.
Obligated
to do it with thoughts of success.

His body glistens. He is not imaginative.

It could not be wrong done that way.
Drifting off the coast, known by
our attention to each other and

the simple details of our clothes.

     Risked everything

     Once able

     Not doubting

the next penny, not bothering to construct
a bridge to it where it glistened as he did
in a deep, square future.

Anchored by the expectation of repetition.
That pink ticket on my car.

    Here is

    I want

    Need you to see me as

    ^ ^ ^

The women flirt with their bodies in words.
Men point the way to the truth. Those elusive
friends cultivate evasiveness. So much is
apparent when work is compared with personality.

Drop down to the next level, where the fish work.
Refuses to quit for the season but we are warm
and dry here, sharing comfortable clothing.

Something happened between those two colors,
a contrast that was jarring. Enough to make it
appear that the colors were in motion.

The rest is details.
But the one thing that you need to know
keeps changing.

Accelerate the process until you find age barreling
through the front door. Wait for no man.

A Filipino walks by, indoors. Rain, still.
No money down, no time to pay, no boys
talking trash at the telephone booth where
we stop for gas.

Back there the water was in turmoil for a long time,
seemed almost unlivable. Those boulders
heaved up on the shore, one right after another.
The boys died or went down swinging. Sometimes
I didn't know what to make of them. No permanence.

Most days fill
with talk
that amounts to little.

"Congratulations on self-restraint, but this
is getting us nowhere."

Do you know anything about why his head spins? Is
her father dead because he wanted to go so badly?
Thin and shapeless. 4:28.

You're his friend. Maybe you should talk to him.
You lead a double life.

       ʌ ʌ ʌ

An enormous oil spill enters the waterway.
Hiding behind this liquid curtain everyone
sees what I cannot.

She said you were extravagant. How can
that magician survive a 10-story fall
into a blazing inferno?

No one said there would be bits of bone.
When we tossed his ashes into the air
I so much wanted things to be right.

I was ignoring how wrong they were.
Then he was no longer there to be corrected.
Who *are* these children?

Time to re-enter the mainstream.
Dislocated people, names that don't fit.
The hokey accents of my place.

How astute do you have to be to know
what's going on?

The numbers in the elevator stacked in a way
that seems entirely illogical.

When people don't give you what you want them to give you,
you turn on them. This is not one of your most endearing
qualities.

How big is his dark side?
You can't get around it.

                    ^ ^ ^

"I am lucky to even be here"
without my phrase book,
having mistaken evil for mischief.

The system is still loaded with values,
although
most are ignored. His creature comforts

provided for in a small cell.
Some who "love" him worry about the narrow width
of his cot. Yet he's asleep, familiar with that hard pillow.

She had no hips. He was mean to her. He lies

on his cot and remembers the implements he used.
They might have drowned together in an inch of water,

a baby forgotten in the tub when the phone rings.
Unmasked, he is something to be afraid of.

They, in their regular old cars, riding around town.
As if my voice were the phony voice of someone else.

This is not normal! Going on the way they go.
I want them all back right now.

The smoke of that circus is colorful, but my friends
are enfolded, muffled in it, gone.

It completes itself whether we offer it guidance or not.
It wins out, even if it does not always make meaning.
Some are crude and ugly. The head of some animal mounted
on the dark paneling of some inner sanctum. These
are not fisherman pleasuring themselves, but hunters.

Bring my boy back with that wholesome smile on his face.
Capture this season before it gets away.

They are riding around town fiddling with their sawed-off
shotguns, not letting us know who they are.

Energy to go out so late at night.
She knew nothing of his dark side.
Memory ripples your surface and I
can't see beneath it. The boat rocks.

When they killed the three of them one after another in those
hot years my life changed forever, even though I do not like to
think I have the sort of dramatic nature that claims such
cataclysm. Their deaths, however, erupted over everything that
I had built. Lava ran down the sides of my shelter. Not senti-

mentality but fear makes my eyes fill up even now when I
allow myself to concentrate on those three men too long.
I am afraid of rage and cool evil.

It adds up swell. He jumped 18 floors into Center Street
and somebody else took the rap.

"On whose evidence was this preposterous warrant issued?"

Her lip is curled but the whole thing was really an accident.
Little did they know.

There's no use pretending – you love me and you know it.

Get going before I change my mind. I suppose you think I'm
nuts.

Very adorable boy sticks his head in the door and will soon
be gone.
The tracks made, accepted by history, just scratch the surface.

Rattle if off like a lost cause. Too soon to put any point on it,
yet who can say.

Improvise us with details, their little turns down the aisles,
preoccupation with sensation.
Teach it how to fix itself under the blue umbrella.

I know more about her body than I want to. Less of his cell.
His rage. Did he keep it under wraps whenever company
called?

His little brothers and sisters out on the skeet shooting range,
taking target practice.
Nothing happens. It's the best thing that could happen.

"You can be what you were before the world betrayed you."

Other children with him.

Oh no, the order is lost.

"Our water is among the purest in the world."

This is what is around me and the suicidal student.

"Reservoirs which protect and hold these pure..."

All burned up in a field in Texas, the children, too, as
emblems of someone's will pitched against someone's will.

∧ ∧ ∧

Moon in an indigo sky, dark clouds
scribbled Chinese writing across,
in transposition and transit.

What I have considered to be important to me
is important.

The house is adorned with candles and butterflies when
the army takes her mother away.

Small goat, embroidered blouse, flowers on a grave.
He loves her (me) so much. *Cuidado.*

Meet me tomorrow night in your house.
Blue room, pink doors, full moon veiled
in ink. May not amount to so much after all.

Half moon halts halfway.

Why this urge to miniaturize
anything exotic. Adhering to its true colors.

The ritual of three squares a day. Our palates
are spoiled.

No false hopes. It's pretty far along and there isn't
much we can do at this stage.

You have been here before. Filled with anxiety,
watching that climb into the sky.

It is my name.

How well do I know you after all
this little time, the length of time they were,
knowing how it is here these days.

Enormous pictures such as "Harmony in Red,"
color locked yet not somnolent. No child would
have invented something so clear and sure in its forms.
Wiggle. Wiggle something.
Deliberately skipped beats unlike the omissions
of anxiety.

I don't know why he is still (yet) so present in
his narrow cot.

Word is that must be made.
Rollicking on the runway between flights,
to make something of it.
Passion in the wings, air as neat as a sob.
Am I close enough, or will it not reach?
Coming into their pool house dripping wet. Self-conscious
about protocol, the smell of leather and pool chemicals, then a

fine restaurant where the settings employ more silverware
than you know how to use. I cannot shake the past even
though the past is shaky, nor fully exile ego from this. Why so
unhappy? For the audience.

Those not here are here and there.

I keep seeing him overcoming her and feeling afraid.

It's like a factory, says one 40-year-old woman who never
got pregnant. Change is a constant.

Songs that hold up.

My every gesture studied as if I were playing professional ball
or running in the Kentucky Derby. It's excruciating.
We are not nations.

My thoughts enclose too much. She inflicts some painful
fictional memory on me that makes me disbelieve. Why allow
that?

If the rhythm is lost and found again,
which action counts more?

Places where touching only what is near them enthralls
the whole body, cannot be done alone.
I prefer to sit near the door.
It's earlier there. Or later. Anyway,
not the same, not
the same vocabulary.
I prefer to sit this one out.
It's done without effect.

Now here we are.

I prefer to stay with it for the time being.

Sensibility was attuned to
a particular city – not this one, yet
as foreign as necessary?
Are the entries obscured, on the basis of experience?

Economics may be murderous.

Can we buy into it? Can we buy into our concern?

∧ ∧ ∧

Was there, but was not the locked room you desired to keep.
Do not speak of the end. Do not speak for it.

I prefer to dwell among you.

Five hours by bus and still not there.
Getting along, though.

Clear liquid balanced to have
a still surface in the long-stemmed blue glass.

The others have made choices when
their plates were put before them. You
help make that possible.

I would prefer not to be steeped in such
lessons from the past.

Already it is quite hot here but people elsewhere
say it is entirely pleasant. If everyone all
at once turned away.
If no one were here exactly.
If the babies had not been, had not come home.
A neighbor heard the window glass shatter.

A policeman saw the flames but saw no one outside.

Carrying the mandolin gently. The boy was drawn
to the old instrument, streaked with soot.

0

What to do but get on with it. He
will not protect you, you should know.

He prefers not to. I prefer the one on the left.

Streets erupt on the television screen. Hollow
boom of exploding electrical wires.

In decline yet still fairly elegant.

You found these words first and shut out
this world.
A ruler and every now and then,
some smart money.

The attractions are almost gone now.
Waiters in tuxedos distribute
whatever they would most like to eat.

A teenage Japanese prince, a retirement home,
all orderly succession. A friend recalls
dandling other women's babies. To this day
we are combing the family records, rooted
in mythic details of dungeons and gardens,
the last places we visited.

The fact is, these events change you forever.

Stands (Adams Morgan)

They're a couple
<color> ruffled waist
bang ruffles, hem, hair ruffled in front

Maria de Buenos Aires
buy trade gold diamond
refillable

Two boys
guys with hair shorn
flat on top

Say it with style
he hangs around
her shoulder a big gold cross

Flores
donde
you don't mean it

To say the verdigris
doors on the church
where the guys lie about

"me too, dear, me too"

Tiny gold earrings
tiny ears
solemn trouper, a believer

Heshe with the long
hair, say, my pants
are long enough and my hat

And my bicycle.
Smile and stride,
speak rapidly

Don't speak – strike
silence in the kids
jewelry, general
Merchandise, bus,
one with copper colored hair
blinking, silent

Police car
cuidado, Aquileo
de pelicula en hora

Microsoft tee shirt
leaning around old phone
barriers,warm
bold look goes
right for the eyes

Now dreaming in Spanish
and still here
a <cowboy> shirt

Paleo mio pink shirt,
pink skirt, *Pepsi cinco*
about the bright red car.

Some latitude attitude
my stand is this
take

Bandera slide across
the front seat, string tie,
por amor a mi pueblo,

orange nails, *tienda santa rosa*
Merenguemania
Tony Acosta y sus amigos

It's school, fat boy,
bueno,
today you stop traffic

Botas en special
Everything must go
chartreuse dress

Small boys with caps
puffed up
boosted blind becoming
trunk full of suitcases
astride those haircuts
Beverly Hills

bopboba bop rhythm
too sweet
for this

tuxedo bib on
albino boy,
gold again.

Respect, posted,
sheltered, wooing.
Strike that.

Chartreuse dress.

Sexy Shoes

1

A fair number of Taiwanese,
Vietnamese, Indonesian refugees
deciding, preferring
not to
get on, get over, get up, get with
prevailing winds and
bulletins,
transfers, transfusions.

Wheat rains
hard and fast,
faster, fasting
spiritual traffic
at ground level
and air, and light.

2

Ingathering at the corner
of siren and dread,
last to join the long list,
secretly pleased by
common language, dancing
the hot step.
No illness, no apathy allowed.
Stripes.
More food than
anyone can possibly in
so little time, more
space than anyone can
rattle around in
less.

Queen

Her teeth
set as perfect arches
white curves under which
a monk might enter
in ghastly habit,
white and white and white
stitched across her wide smile.
Back behind those teeth
where do we go, if we go,
into an unknown space
her thoughts, spun across
the barren landscape
of her past, cast off or
whitewashed by boys
she hires for
her dirtywork. Every-
one has dirtywork,
she thinks.

      The parade
of tin lizzies lasts
only an hour before
the conventional cars
zoom ahead. Her teeth
clack-clack-clack
at the finish where
she awards ribbons
to the winners, her shining
mother watching the event,
dust-covered and smiling,
with her own teeth,
in pleasure and abandon.

Hurling Across the Plains

Sherene looked out her window and saw
a man beating the teeth right out of a woman

The two-year-old boy taken dead
to the hospital, a spoon
shoved down his throat, past broken teeth

A blonde and a black
A blonde and a black

A dozen smart doctors, most of them
women

Green as a lozenge or a bar
of translucent soap, protected by cloud cover

Adorable baby, quiet all during our descent

Clouds turn over outside of his grasp,
eggs, the unborn

Fabric to be laid out on a table and cut to shape
later

Sorry doll, so sorry

One is a star and does not move.

MORE

When We Were Violent

The elusive optimism
skin of ice on the pond
early morning
all water by noon.

Imagine a different fate
one less repetitive
mild insistence pursuing
the same mistaken path.

When we were violent they were more violent so we became
still more violent until all of the rocks and blades were gone
over to the other side for further use and so on and so forth
and so on.

Tantrum

Bellyfish lobster-lolly
craydaddy bang
hoopla benny burden
crack crinkle spine

Big bobba loo day
kick crappy foo
still wagon crash kickel
ordnance fray

clap doodle fringe telly
slap saddle groan
B-52 bomber
kiss kettle throne

Trijicon night sites
Tactical knives
Cherokee cheek-piece
R.A.T.S. lesser sights

Laser grips, Choate stocks
ASP Batons
Gerber knives Blackhawks
Beta-C Mags

Raptor weapon bays
Phantom Corsair
hardpoints Tigershark
F-35

Super Hornet payload
Buccaneer Mirage
Nighthawk Terminator
Little Bird Chinook

Booby-Trap Hornet
Lancer Tigershark
Cobra Apache
Beretta Sentry Prowler

Osprey Atlas
ICBM
Centaur hydrazine
Dragon Javelin

Bushmaster Chain Gun
Walther carbine
Grenade launcher Browning
M16

Kalashnikov Tomahawk
Bradleys Abrams Scout
Peacekeeper Gatling
Sparrow Phoenix Harm

Polaris Poseidon
Nike Stinger SLAM
M4 MP5
Maverick Harpoon

ASROC Albatross
Eagle Stratofortress
Brimstone Bullpup
Bantam Chapparral

Condor Copperhead
CBSS
Delilah Elbrus
Enzian Frog-5

Feuerlilie Gadfly
Gopher Global Shadow

Hound Dog Iris-T
Jericho Koala

Kormoran Kingfish
Little John Lizard
Longbow Minuteman
Mistral Navaho

Otomat Patriot
Pershing Pioneer
Quad-50 Redstone
Rheinbote Saddler

Shipwreck Scamp Shturm
Seawolf Shillelagh
Sandbox Scapegoat
Stratotanker Sentry

Stallion Standard
Spanker Spartan Spider
Starburst Trident
Type 64

Ural Volga Vulcan
Walleye X1
Yozh ZT-3 Swift
Zippo Boats Zyb

Bellyfish lobster-lolly
craydaddy bang
hoopla benny burden
crick crackle spine

Kickapoo joy juice
blood orange spew
body bag depot
baby come too.

Car Trip: Eastern Maryland

Behind a shield from wind, beside him,
holding his hand. No standard but acceptance
rules the margins of visibility.

A ledge of thought on which he or she
or someone else is poised.

How might that threaten the rift
in the trees, overlarge leaves,
hands wide open, tremulous at the lip
of that ledge.
           On the way out of town,
along the narrow blocks surrendered
to the poor. A brown skinned man and woman
carrying bulging plastic sacks
of laundry on their heads cross Irving Street.

What is it that makes
the *thought* thing the *said* thing?
Why doesn't all of it get said?

The mimosas are blooming,
and the Rose of Sharon.

I always characterize you as sweet
and special, (*move closer*) and I save
all the notes you write to me.

The clouds look wholesome, very white and
puffed up, edible.

At the funeral he appeared
uncomfortable with being a person, as if
he wanted to return to his animal home.

A life of blowing up relationships
all along the way, leaving a wake
of pots and pans and rowing machines,
address books tossed out.

Out walking in a natural setting but
they are all wearing headphones.
Her difficult visit, her delight in us.
Now she is addled but we all love her
and answer every repetitive question.

Crossing a blue band of water
that glitters, as the bridge rails
glitter where the sun hits them.

This is the town where her family
had put down roots. She keeps her own
counsel now that her brother and sister
both are gone.
           She's become a mother
almost on her own. Her mother looks after
her face, still has a melodious laugh.

Who takes these boats out on the South River,
leaving a little trail of gasoline
on the surface of the water?

They did not know what they were doing
but they always had a really good time.

Does a Buick look better in Wisconsin?

Single family homes on a flatland.

A farmhouse under a stand of trees
making shade for it.

Straight ahead, a sign for Hope. Fifteen miles
east to The Bay Bridge. This map
does not show every point that interests us.

Long trailers filled with name brand
chickens.
        Being here and happy about it,
making an orderly garden, a mix of flowers
and vegetables, green vines climbing a trellis.

A tinge of pink in the clouds now,
indicating afternoon.

Suddenly the water appears behind these
shingled houses, wide and calm.

I was not careful of his feelings.

Give me the money to build my church.
So they have done. In multiples.
Trust your luck.

Queenstown junction with 301.

What signals the start of a habit?
A softshell crab sandwich,
a habitual meeting place, a word
that by its habitual use becomes a
comforting gesture.

The filaments in an ordinary bulb
glow like the embers of a twig or a cigarette.

I have put all my junk out in the yard
for you to look at and think about.

Wearing clothes they've made themselves, those
unusual matching prints a dead giveaway.

Balloons for someone's birthday.
An education that lacks breadth and depth
but that imparts a high polish to the bearer.
She is still so lovely.

Waiting to be fed or preparing
food for others. Refilling the ice tray
and carrying it carefully
across the kitchen floor to the freezer.

Unable to solve the family or to find
the comforting gesture of a word that does not
require understanding.

I have to make him his mashed potatoes now
with turkey gravy.

I did not have it in mind to go back there.

Water Between an Inner and an Outer Hull

Somehow keeps the ship afloat.
Kindness, the first time I felt
a man's hand gentle the back
of my neck, heat all through my body.

Circling an oak tree so he wouldn't see
me.
    Now a small boy swoops around
my happiness, so much to be told.

Not all forward motion, but much of it.
Do the two of us
make other people happy now?
Have we become gatherers, at peace with fate?

Another cinderblock room, for sleeping only,
without stored bottles of water or prayer books.

My cousin
at the piano already dreaming
his unspeakable dreams.

My aunt never dreaming her getaway,
or what got away from all of them.

The boy in the backyard, humming
his tunes discordantly, rocking back and forth
on his perch on a basement window sill.

The heat and stillness of the air there,
wanting to press the green mulberry leaves against
your face, against all that's exposed. Relief.

I'm too tired to imitate anyone else right now
but I stay slowly and trust that gesture.

Irony and distance depart from the form.

Familiar Song

Does he ever feel bad
that what was wrong
with him became what
was wrong with her?

A man high-stepping through snow
or someone out of view signaled
only by a white handkerchief
waved languidly as
a steamer leaves port.

Pretend we are married
or once were in front
of a gallery of old friends.
This towel
becomes your towel and now
it is home:
your bureau, your closet,
your side of the bed.

I don't want ceremony in
a torrid climate under
slow-turning fans. What
could I read now
and understand better
than when I read it before?

I see what's coming
before he sees it. To be
in a strange place with
these people worried
about missing the point.
Am I depressed? To be
in a strange place with –

These people on board,
none of whom knows
the songs I know, each one
hungrier than the others imagine,
surrounded by these strange
people, none of whom knows
my songs or my place. We set sail.

Suddenly there are Mary and Charlie.

Your Water Is Expired

Anthrax alert. You're wanted in
some other matters.
Cops toss the mattress,
the room. I've begun
to wonder if 112000
makes sense:
is the address realistic?
I'm sorry I didn't hear you
maybe it is doomsday right
here right now.

*

We were all in one room
We couldn't agree on anything
or confront one another.

A party affiliation,
a horde of third world nations
that surround America,
mongrels of the world unite.

A vanished vocabulary
for friends who come and go
like rock bands, or bands of
terriers on the go, barking
some shrill new word.

Better anticipate
a drenching rain before sleep
crazed with dreams.

Friends are sold out,
brilliantly directed
into their own small businesses,

given a line of credit, offered
more space than a Mercedes 320.
It's like that
on an ordinary Tuesday night.

The other dog dreams
he's in the band, his sleep
vanishes, he wakes, drenched.

Genes

I come from
A family of artists
And bedwetters.
I wanted to be
Poor but honest,
But it didn't work out.

The style was all wrong.
The men walked off the job
Before the vegans could be fed
Or the egoists mollified.
We all went off in a huff,
In a babble, a brocade of tongues.

When I awoke
An elegant voice
Was speaking in my head
In a vocabulary little like my own.
I wrote down everything
It had to say
And signed my name to it.

Ideas

Today's word is cool,
tomorrow's is children.

Whatever ideas get through
will be altered, bronzed or
blackened before
the end of the century.

Lights dim
and brighten again,
the ritual of blinking.

The boys run and run
legs lift high
over the macadam,
keep going, scraped
knees and all.

Smoking

I could not stop smoking, not for many years.
That sweet smell, that companion.

That sweet man, his very English name,
Like Mrs. Brittingham's.

As real as the bridge that crosses Howard Street,
now painted bright red as if it is something
new, some serious sculpture.

I threw my cigarette out the window
but it came in the back window and set
the car on fire. People honked
and pointed as I drove by. Puzzled,
I waved back.

Bright red girders, so
ashamed of your own words.

Things Not To Talk About:

children
hosiery
upholstery
laundry
that time of the month

jewelry
money
jealousy
doubt
failure

knitting
Quebec
the Stork Club
recycling
cheating

I invent your eyes
to look at me
in judgment
as I set the soundtrack
to one sad album
on "repeat"

don't be ashamed

it's just time
to go back to Baltimore now.

Everyone bites the hand–
some know it and apologize

knowing others may not read this
as you do, may not see in it
what I do, and that it does not matter.

am not you, but am enough,
am eminent.

∧

Friends come into something
of their own,
and more accomplished
lives than I'd have guessed.

And tests and liabilities
children and infirmities
secrets and lies, although
that's really no surprise,
(I rhyme here
just like my grandfather,
oh dear.)

And endings, too,
the roster changes, naming
the unknown

capable of learning or change
disrupting the rhythm
on a long flight from here
to here we are again.

You attach yourself to
the body in this way–
understandable,
but foolish perhaps.

I love my bed
now
I love my bed

The director draws our attention
to his folded hands, the player's
folded hands, a pointed clue
I can't help but ignore.

Simply There

I effect a new principle
for scissors that appear
in memory for no reason.

Do not negate the thought
of Alice's stars
streaming past the window
during this restless flight.

He denies that his hair
Was ever that long
But I remember cutting it away
From his collar late,
late at night.

Memory is stronger,
weaker.

I thought she knew.

When is the time of change
coming to an end.
When is the conversation
at rest.
What story
What notion
What catastrophe tumbles
the chimneys like that.

Roasted or thrust under
the brushes.

How can I explain
how familiar it is.

Tina is there
in the snow or in a storm,
or simply there.

It is all there just
as it was before:
the quadrant,
the space shuttle,
the murder at Altamont.

Set With Furniture

Pasha fights off pneumonia,
dreaming the souls of carriages.

Furniture breaks my heart
precipitous,
proving undependable.

It's a matter of safety
soon to be obsolete
as the individual discards
identity in favor
of stock options.

The furniture leaps into space
with a taut grace, suspending itself
on a strong rope from
the rafters in the garage,
won't go, won't be lost.

An idea captured in skin
like a life of its own,
barricaded like that.

This is not ouch-free.
Sometimes it hurts more
in spite of practice.

I solo this part
and I don't like it.

∧

This year's question
opposes
last year's: why
does any of it get said?

You tell me.

Yes, I believe
that carriages have souls.

Out in the rain today
a mother worries, runs
between drops.

Falling like that I
don't know why he did
to explore
what
and why
no one heard
the big noise of his going.

Can you abandon any of them,
these ideas heavy
with responsibility, to
let go might be—

I know someone
whose parrot speaks
only words from *Finnegan's Wake.*
He waits for his interview,
he bides his time,
braids his line,
bleeds his wine.

I imagine something noble
about a seal
balancing a ball on its nose,
no humor there.
But not so noble
for a man to do that.

Hark, hark, the dogs do bark.

Not a world
of calendars and clocks,
makes it hard
to figure out what you've wasted.

∧

The second one is so much better.
Yes, but it doesn't mean more
than paper or plastic.

The duck comes down.
You win a hundred dollars.

and get right on with it
still trying
to remember
the name you were born with.

for Pavel Makov

Dot Dot Dot…

From the air a cloverleaf,
furrows of jet trails
loop over The Loop.
Not so radical, really.

I look forward
to seeing you again
in low visibility
(four dots fly over that word
as I look back).

Mockba

Soap is soap
Bread is bread
Car is car
Thief is thief
Train is train
Stone is stone
Say is say
Tell is tell
Time is time
Hot is hot
Fly is fly
Money is money
Rain is rain
Dirt is dirt
Dog is dog

for Dennis O'Neil

Home as It Is

After *The Giant with the Threee Golden Hairs*
— a Russian fairy tale

A road paved with shooting stars,
Vantage point:
Prairie smoke that climbs
A mountain, a mountain moving west
In a shroud of clouds.

In the palace of the unborn
Near the crest of that mountain
A daughter sleeps in the shade
Of a green parasol, on a bed
Of yarrow and sweet marjoram.

The path at her door winds
Seven leagues to an old woman, her
Cottage covered in bindweed and morning glory.
Her six, sleek intelligent dogs are at rest,
Having cancelled the King's curse.

Round the cottage
A hedge of briars grows
So that none can discover its beauty,
No daughter, not even those who follow
The old woman's trail of bright petals.

On a far off plain, a battle rages.
By the sea, a fisherman
Talks to his catch. In the forest
A huntsman whittles a wife,
A branch taken from the tree of golden apples.

When the King returns
He wears a shepherd's tattered smock
And begs a plate of food.
"I have acted incautiously," he says,
"But from no bad motive."

A marriage is celebrated,
A baby squalls, a gale
Blows through the empty town,
Leaves tremble in the wood,
The King's heart grows still more tender.

In a garden, three robbers
Open a letter. At daybreak the first
Sunbeams shed light on joy.
The robbers weep, then decide
To reverse the course of things so far.

for Pasha , and for Alyona Kirtsova

Shopping

Out of breath
        Fear in
Chechen classrooms

Pavé heart charm
Second eruption imminent

Pin in the map
Angry

Breakfast
Cereal suspects in
Neglected areas

Cancer
Fancy seasonal shoes

Very Saks
Very Bergdorf

Wedding pages
Trial by
Faded hopes forces
Kill 9

Future of tension between
Your jewelry and the allies

Bigger eruption enduring
Shoes, coats on 3

Never boring
Never bored.

Odds Over Evens

So readable, a face
I wish I could
embrace that young boy
you were,
and this and that.

Lace lying on the fields
far from our frustrations.
Snow geese there a white
blanket on corn stubble.
Everything smoothes out.

Lotion after a warm soak,
letter from a friend,
glass of sherry.

Lamp, folding table, clear
surface, a walk on
the wild side
without leaving the house.

TIME

Jackpot!

Air frees itself in these cold days – get it?

Everything now reminds me
Of something I used to have, love, see, believe,
Envy, dislike, fear, enjoy, dread, sleep with.

How did I get to be a Jew in America?
Getting on with laughter
As a way of life that turns away from all
The grim then and now.

What do I know about Darfur?
All right to say "I"?

*Sorry, I'm not in the mood for a party tonight, I'm
going out to celebrate quietly on my own.*
Gathering of rags, enormous bellies, flies.
Mind that! Leave it!
The connection, blasted,
Reconfigures the map.

Intersecting circles, a network
Of experience and ideas,
The bus
I like it here. But I'll be moving soon.
Is late. We leap some dirty banks
Of snow to board, then gasp
Down the street. *You know, sir you're*
A bit depressed for a man on his birthday.

Does the tiger regret his snarl?
Does the Challenger evaporate?

Tender numbers, years all wet
And trim as we were telling you.

A carton of cotillions
Wracked with debutantes.
Whirling in dramatic license.
The boys kin to waves of violence, drinking
Leaves from the bottoms of cups
Before anything is told.

To me you're nothing but a dirty joke.
Dusty or muddy depending on the season.
Have you been practicing?

Roars again with no regret. Time
Tips overboard, flag sails,
Small daughters smitten with menace.

Unearthed from under the sacred asphalt where
The Yaqui perform the deer dance.
"Sit down" appends a paper question to
The cellophane briefcase,
Drives the aching bus through snow.

Caged with his long teeth
And a small drum.
When it is gone where
Shall we look – in the May diary?
In a magazine called *"Gladiola"*?

Three enters, one a true calling.
So oriented toward the story,
I missed the beauty of
Camera angles, lines as long as
Words for nothing but
A trillion stars at least.

Appeal, applause, apply
Truth in the well-lit exits.
Flock of particulars
Lists, yaws right here at home
Or on the cracked dry dirt.

Jackpot or half a word
As the day grows old
Just lying about, half-
Listening to the drift of things.

Worlds upon worlds and whirls
Away from the bottleneck.

Jackpot!

Wonder world once
A taste for everywhere
And everything at once,
Koala bears, Laplanders,
Headhunters, zebras,
The Mysterious East.

Shriveled and shrunken
To this ball on a string.
Boxed and ribboned
Its shiny fleet rocked on blue water
Dawn slipped over the wings, Earth
Rising. Magnificent.

Men in the late night tube, eyes
Closed, the women,
Vigilant, boxed and ribboned.

Rich wags runted and absolved
Determine a space between those Old – these New.

Another able desert crossing
In sand and contentment.
The drink or something other,
Do you remember?
Lousy luck, or an accident
Shrill with carelessness.
Throw no roses.
Become a routine fixture
On the scene, a bill of sale,
Stopwatch found on the side of the road
An empty seat in the now empty bus.

The guns ready for transport. Roads
Newly paved for the oligarchy
In support of _____.

Wishing will not make it so
Nor another trip into the desert
Casting a skein of fine webbing
To contain _____.
Retreating into argument.

The wish to associate blindly with
Other manufacturers, with potentates and
Anonymous donors, the ones to watch
Over women and children
Measuring fabric in a loft with
Asian men who lick the air in Canton.

It zips past as David Byrne
Or Philip Glass
Spun into Muzak long ago.
Pulls for the Southern tip as
A creed, a crescent, a gap in credibility.

Focus a light on the man in the suit,
Only *Because I believe that the world...*
Because I believe ...that the world...
Because I believe that the world...
As he was saying...as

for Doug Lang

Quoted passages from *The Birthday Party,*
—Harold Pinter

A Year

Is that it? Are we
all finished now?
Does it come with a warranty?
As much put in as taken out
as much or more to carry now
with an expectation of limits
on time, on guarantees,
on a way of looking at things.
To be bold enough to go there
I adopted
sleep as a pastime and companion
blanketed in a foggy understanding
of what I had to do next.
Little things fell away
like pebbles shaken out of a shoe
and striding on
hand in hand with my own ghost,
getting to know each other, making friends
or not quite – more an acknowledgment,
our body a single we curl up in.

When You Are Lucky Enough
to Get the Red One

Trembles, glows
finally just tastes good
and does not catch fire
or point the way to loss
getting by after the carpenter's
accident, numbing chairs
in the hospital corridor
knew the news might
be good
the nurse rubbed her back
a sticking moment
can't shake it out
like salt and sugar
at the beach house in damp
weather, like that red candy
stuck in its wrapper.

Begin at Once

Crab cake sandwich, cole slaw
and ice tea.

I'll be right back if that's okay.
Big dinner tonight.

Banana cream pie.
German chocolate cheesecake.

Two kinds of strawberry things.
Anything with strawberries on top.

Can we get the whole pie?

People who used to be hungry
sit down now, begin at once.

        &

After that millennium is another
in the matched set so big you
can't get a room around it, a whole house.

Seasoned travelers beseech me
to have a go at it so I go at it.

Children of adults return
to civilization unfettered,
trampling the barricades

as if they were mere petals or blossoms.
I intend you no harm

nor can I imagine what harm

would come of any mistakes we might make,
even conjointly, when each of us

is so obviously well-intentioned.

Decide to quiver then
ignore that instruction.

Leaves are being put through their paces
while I sit here editing
a sermon on miracles.

Deprived of my beliefs I later
began to believe more fervently
in something that was even more true.

I believe
that remaining hopeful is admirable.

      &

Do we go into the hot tub
without our clothes?

I have a number of questions I
meant to ask earlier.

      In the process of getting to know
      each other
      Laurette and I exchange information.
      She likes to ski, is getting married
      in November.

I saw rubber stamps that make
tiny prints of animals' paws and hooves.

"The tips of her shoes drag across
the snow."

        &&

There are not so many windows
into this world

no opening to depend on,
all it goes is slowly,

sometimes heavenward,
with no escorting angels.

Places are left at the table
set habitually for eight.
The evening spirals down.
Snow dusts his wine glass

at first, then
settles in the bowl.

The curtains have been drawn
across windows without openings.

        &&

The music they insist on playing
is louder than I like,

and so rhythmic that it interferes
with my brainwaves,

sets up
new unlikable patterns.

Each seat in the hot tub
massages a different

part of your anatomy.
It is miraculous.

       &

Whether to feather a nest or keep
on the wing, as it were, one goes.

Not bird sounds but car alarms
at the start of every day.

It is enough of this now.
I want to live in that place

where things happen for a reason.
So little in our hands, why

make plans? I nail the past in place,
then see how boring it is.

None of this is correct anymore.
It is old; the computer is old.

They recommend wearing red but
the color jumps out of the lines.

Not easy to get to the altar either,
leaping the obstacles in the marriage

bureau department of motor vehicles
and tax adjustments.

&

You wake up late.
The printouts stretch

all the way across the floor. Your
name is missing. The labels

aren't sticky enough. The trees
are turning from the top down.

Your younger replicas, those versions,
take the streets.

The play is performed without you—
it seems like a miracle.

We stayed at a replica
of a five-day rental for two days.

It was Southern so it seemed
friendly and sinister all at once,

like windows that have been painted
an opaque dark green.
It is enough of this now.
These tactics only contribute
paradox to being and nothingness.

        Laurette colors the dark place
        a lighter shade
        but it does not stop time.
        Laurette cannot.

She exits to the hot tub, to the altar,
to a limousine that waits outside
with all the drinks in its bar
already drunk up and all the glasses

greasy with lipstains, the floor
littered with crumpled napkins.

       &

Wear something blue for contrast.
Wear pearls over that.

So much is constructed to assist us,
in not being where we are

telephone, television, telegraph,
telepathy, telescopes

and relationships that require
long distance transportation.

            I have not yet done the taping.
            I have done the taping.
            It has not yet aired.
            It has aired.

"I had to achieve accuracy to almost
100% in the work that I did.
You too. That's to our advantage."
"I have to write down everything
because I don't want to remember
these things. I throw a note

on the floor in the kitchen so
I won't forget where I put it."

&

Finally I settled for his being
willing to do everything I said.
But it was not enough, a bad trade.

Wasn't she supposed to be
an ingenue forever?
No.

I hate the forced-higher, brighter,
bigger voices of little musical
theater stars, those ingenues, those girls.

&

A popular airplane for
commuter airlines has crashed
in a cornfield, a cornfield.

I hear your car alarm wailing
without you. Maybe you'd better
go outside, take a look.

Late at night when I'm alone
in a dark place I see you kissing
someone else. I make you kiss her.

Oh those ingenues, those girls!
The tips of their shoes drag across
the snow.

&

The natural beauty of the nightmare
gathered under the comforter,
sheltered in star patterns,

log cabins, flying geese.
Winter winnows weak from strong
in honor of missing children.

Being as lonely as that in the snow
in the center of a room of four
stone walls, and opaque windows.

Keys rattle, clinging together as
the door is locked.
Its little glass knob won't turn.

A bird and a flower, either one,
especially in combination with vines,
usually on porcelain, in deep
warm tones –

these are you
in my mind,

like the cup that rests, broken,
behind the toaster, too
graceful to discard.

I like geometry. We both favor
what's real.
The tips of their shoes.

My cigarette, my wine,
my end of the line.

Now the bed is trembling.
Now the window rattles in its frame.

Now I want
to stay here a while
on the trembling bed.

Change at the Gate

A series of goodbyes
wire and airplanes
with so much heat
we missed them all.

Change at the gate
a late arrival
all boxes draped
in a falsehood.

Where was the name
on the map as a cipher
a pig in a poke
telescoped and telegraphed

The longed for
like a military song,
brass music, chopped up
into a 21 gun salute

My country welcomes you
like a mid-level cowboy
reading a book
on an airplane

Following our
fragile grandmothers,
flames on Primrose Lane
let me explain:

It is mine and
it is yours and may
become as valuable
as a cardinal.

Yet because I taught you
the wrong words you
must stay here now,
evading questions.

Swinging from vines
or familial attachments
chained to another land
a quizzical father.

You can do
with your life
whatever you want –
perhaps not here.

Now "this"
is your "home" even if
not "home" even if
made of fire

all fire and air
like a scratchy soundtrack or
the tracks of a convoy
that betrays your purpose here

You cannot know
what time remembers
or may wish
to bring you toward

Trips

Trips over seas (it's
the sea that touches a sea that touches
a sea, one sea, straits float
the Fish, bring snails
from Creation to the Dimming) leaning
on the rail at its end, speaking of a trip
(these words alone can
madden from longing)

BIO NOTE

Beth Joselow has been writing poems all her life. She has
been publishing poetry, prose and plays since her early
twenties, and her work has appeared in numerous
magazines and anthologies. She often has worked with
artists and musicians. Three of her poems were composed
into a song-cycle by Janet Peachy. Her collaboration on
an artists book with the Russian artist Pavel Makov was
chosen for the Osaka Triennial in the late 1990s. Her plays
have been staged in New York and Washington DC. *Begin
At Once* is her eighth book of poems. Others include *The
April Wars, Broad Daylight, Excontemporary, Self-Regard*,
and *The Bottleneck*.

For many years, Beth Joselow taught on the faculty
of the Corcoran School of Art + Design. She is now
a psychotherapist working mostly with children. She
lives near the Atlantic Ocean in Lewes DE with her
husband and a large dog.

OTHER BOOKS FROM CHAX PRESS

Glen Mott, *Analects on a Chinese Screen*
Tim Peterson, *Since I Moved In*
Linda Russo, *Mirth*
Jefferson Carter, *Sentimental Blue*
Charles Borkhuis, *Afterimage*
Bruce Andrews, *Swoon Noir*
Joe Amato, *Under Virga*
David Abel, *Black Valentine*
Paul Naylor, *Arranging Nature*
Kass Fleisher, *Accidental Species*
Tenney Nathanson, *Erased Art*
Heather Nagami, *Hostile*
Linh Dinh, *American Tatts*
Patrick Pritchett, *Burn: Doxology for Joan of Arc*
Jonathan Brannen, *Deaccessioned Landscapes*
Beverly Dahlen, *A-Reading Spicer & 18 Sonnets*
Elizabeth Treadwell, *Chantry*

For our many additional titles please visit our web site:
http://www.chax.org/

Chax Press is supported by the Tucson Pima Arts Council and by the
Arizona Commission on the Arts with funding from the State of
Arizona and the National Endowment for the Arts.